"In turns elegiac, documentary, and c‹
allowed her fervent meditations to be overheard, and has thereby
enlisted us in joining a prayerful dialogue with the God, and with
one another. At every turn, she manifests an understanding that
the poetic operation of language—those parabolic structures that
allow our speaking more than we know to say—is one's best path
to apprehending within the Most a surpassing All."

    —**Scott Cairns**, author of *Slow Pilgrim: The Collected Poems*

"For one seeking to come out from the darkness and into the
light, that journey could well begin and end with Baumgaertner's
new book. Her poems remind me that words on a page harbor
and invite the divine Word; that the poem can be crucible and
crucifix to fix and transfix the eternal; that the destination of all
our journeys is to shuck the seeds of shade inside us and enter fully
into the shine of His light."

    —**Valerie Wohlfeld**, chosen for the Yale Series of Younger Poets Prize

"Here is bread to feed the hungry soul with words that truly
matter, words which will bring you closer to Christ, the Incarnate
Word, the One who 'rises, /he rises indeed,/light blazing.' Oh,
and the places she evokes with such heartbreaking accuracy—the
Concentration Camps, Cuba, and for me especially those ancient
runes of history in the way she captures the Orkneys. And so much
more: marriage, that long-lost life of aunts and uncles and devout
musicians and a dear bull terrier who live now in vibrant memory.
Read her as you would the Psalms and those Metaphysical poets
she so beautifully echoes. You too will be uplifted by her words,
her music, her presence."

    —**Paul Mariani**, author of *The Mystery of It All: The Vocation of Poetry
in the Twilight of Modernity*

"There is an exhilarating permanence about Baumgaertner's remarkable poems. Hands cupped to receive the Eucharist are said, in one poem, to be 'a small manger'—for Christians, a stunning and deeply true picture; there are plenty of others. The images and music of these poems bear steady witness to God's abiding presence and love, even as the poems engagingly address widely various subjects. These are tough-minded poems of faith and hope, and they couldn't have come at a better time."
— **Charles Hughes,** author of *The Evening Sky* and *Cave Art*

"Baumgaertner has long been a voice crying in the wilderness, calling us to embrace poetry of beauty, goodness, and the mysterious truths of Christian faith. Here, she takes us on journeys back to her ancestral Cuba, to the horrors of Nazi-crushed Poland, to the earliest days of life beyond the garden with Eve and her family, to the ancient and rugged coast of Scotland's Orkney Islands, and to current-day America. She converses with diverse poets—even out-smarting Christopher Smart with her dog Maddie usurping the place previously held by a cat named Jeoffrey. Perhaps Baumgaertner's richest gifts to us, though, are in her liturgical poems. How wise church leaders would be to draw these poems into the life of their communities."
— **D.S. Martin,** author of *Angelicus,* and Poet-in-Residence at McMaster Divinity College

"For all our effort, we may never get the meaning of past and present, the nature of beauty or savagery, or the relationship of God and the world right. To live thoughtfully and devoutly in time is, in a sense, to be in perpetual risk of heresy; the most we can hope is, from time to time, to get such things less wrong. Baumgaertner's new poems are meditations of fine detail and great beauty that lead us into the mystery of the world and the mystery of the divine and, in their unfailing honesty, somehow leave us less wrong about these things than we were before."
— **James Matthew Wilson,** author of *The Strangeness of the Good*

NEW POEMS

From Shade to Shine

JILL PELÁEZ BAUMGAERTNER

IRON
PEN

PARACLETE PRESS
BREWSTER, MASSACHUSETTS

For
London, Zoe, Cayd, and Zola

2022 First Printing

From Shade to Shine: New Poems

Copyright © 2022 by Jill Peláez Baumgaertner

ISBN 978-1-64060-598-5

The Iron Pen name and logo are trademarks of Paraclete Press.

Library of Congress Control Number: 2021953538

10 9 8 7 6 5 4 3 2 1

Published by Paraclete Press
Brewster, Massachusetts
www.paracletepress.com

Printed in the United States of America

The Quidditie

My God, a verse is not a crown,
    No point of honour, or gay suit,
No hawk, or banquet, or renown,
    Nor a good sword, nor yet a lute.

It cannot vault, or dance, or play;
    It never was in France or Spain;
Nor can it entertain the day
    With a great stable or domain.

It is no office, art, or news;
    Nor the Exchange, or busy Hall:
But it is that which, while I use,
    I am with Thee, and *Most take all.*

—GEORGE HERBERT

CONTENTS

PROLOGUE

—— I ——

—— *Magdalene* POEMS ——

—— *Mary* SONGS ——

—— II ——

—— III ——

PROLOGUE

Meditation on Psalm 8

O LORD our Lord
how exalted is your name in all the world!

A name like no other,
God, you are on our lips,
your name in our throats,
the syllables filling, substantial
like bread on our tongues.
We cannot get enough of you.
You kindle our glee
and tame our grief,
propel our metaphors,
invade our songs.
Even when it is not our intention
to put you there, you are there.
For you the moon and stars
are mere fingertoys, and you
spin them like gyroscopes.
And here we sit in the turn
of creation, our minds agape,
stupefied by your love for us.

What are we in comparison
to all that you have made?
You have strewn us
with a profusion of blossoms,
an abundance of sunlight.
Only the angels and you,
the Lord of the Universe,
are closer to heaven.

You have given us
this earth and time on it.
All house painters and finger painters,
teachers and designers,

all coaches and men working in trees,
all gymnasts defying gravity,
cooks and midwives,
grandparents with their eyes
on the generations.
You have crafted us
like sculpture
and painted the world
with colors only
you can name,
you whose name
is so like no other
it hallows our throats
when its syllables
form on our lips.

— I —

Poem for November

Ephesians 5:8–20

Many trees are mere stencils now,
but some still dazzle, those with light
in their yellow leaves, this even
as November skies stretch mute
and somber.

It is easy this time of year
to dwell on losses and the world
so shattered, even watching this translucent
yellow tree, whose light one could read by,
this blaze against the dimming season.

And we are gathered, each one of us,
in this autumn dilemma,
both anchored and adrift.

Like Eve reaching for Adam's hand
as they stand, stunned,
outside the gates.

Or that child, Mary, who in the silence
after Gabriel's startling news,
wonders, "Should I say yes?"

Or Paul, the persecutor, eyes scaled,
his mouth a thin, straight
line, his heart in its first
ever motion of turning over.

Or two thousand years later
those rabbis at Auschwitz
who put God on trial,
convicted him,
then turned to evening prayer.

Or the aging professor
who said that when he cannot
forgive, he simply acts as if he had.

These images may seem splinters,
fragments scattered and aimless.
But we are not so twisted
that we cannot see the cross's
change from torture into bliss,
from blood and slivers
into the gleam of polished
planks for Christ, arms
raised in victory.

So here we gather
in all of our imperfections,
waiting for song to blaze into the dark
corners, as this year races
toward both finales and preludes.

Listen. Soon one clear voice will blend
with another. Anchored by the rush
of melody we will catch hold
of the whole breath and timbre
of the moment and together
in this world so prone to drift,
we will see by the cross,
the tree of light, pure music.

Advent

That breathless moment before the maestro
raises the baton, before the leaf falls,
before the page turns—

Just as the music begins to begin,
the leaf loosens its hold,
the words on the page give way
to more pages—

His coming is prelude, our waiting
for the fullness of time, a double waiting.

The Word Made Flesh

The Word which shaped
creation's air, dust-spinning,
sea-gathering, clay-carving,
life-sparking.

This Word more than
the wisp of syllables, its
gospel-making sweeter
than voicing.

Dark-shattered light,
revealed Word, letter perfect,
sight-giving, visible,
bright fleshprint.

This birth-marked Word,
sense-opening, how can such
spirit dwell in a child's
shallow breath?

Christmas

He comes small as slender silence,
still as mist,
breath soft as feather float,
not for birth's sake born
but for our washing and our feeding.
An immensity of Word,
this infant lowly stabled,
whose voice could shake the wilderness,
uproot cedars,
strip the forest bare,
here breathes air crisp as the skin of snow
and sleeps on hay.

Epiphany

The eyeless dark of mole, worm, coffin.
Earth snugs them. Small breathing
or none. But then the light from Magi's
star's first gleam and sign, the gloom
transformed from shade to shine.
Light streaming. Deep, full breathing.
Eyes muscled open. And Christ at first
a fog, a blur. Enigma. But then arms raised,
so clearly Christus Victor.

Ash Wednesday

In memoriam, Anya Silver

We chose not to see
how close it hovered.
She had been sick so long
we had grown accustomed
to her bright scarves
and turbans as she sipped
her drink across the table
or read her poems
behind the podium,
such shakings, such delicacy.

She told the poets gathered
that her favorite season was Lent.
"It is a great comfort," she said,
"Ashes to ashes a reminder
that everyone, each
in their chosen pew, is dying."

And now her digitized voice
only bits in the cloud,
her face a flicker of light and dark
on screens, except her poems
where words have
the resonance of absence.

Even buried, bones live, motionless,
for many more years than
the body has breath,
and so her words

and the crumbling to ash,
soot and oil on the pastor's fingers.

Sitting in our pews
we breathe in the dissolution,
John Donne says, of royalty and pauper,
their mouths filled with dust,
our mouths filled with their dust.

Tempter/Redemptor

Turn stone to bread.
Soften granite to crust,
pebbles to crumbs,
obsidian to dough.

The stunt is all
the bread this hunger grows,
a trick, a stratagem
the Host declines.

Vault from the parapet.
Boast the thrill
of hurtling straight
into the angels' arms,
a leap of faith
to test God's love.

No vertigo,
his balance perfect,
this unswerving Christ,
hands stretched,
feet fixed.

The devil claims the cities,
Stock exchange, the throne.
All this he tenders for one bow.

Christ kneels but not to brawn
or guile. He bows
to power, mystery,
to light without shadow,
to love as dazzling as pain.

Lent

Here there is no alone.
In the garden of ashes the dust
poured from urns mixes
with dust poured from all urns.
We die alone, yet we all die,
mingled as one.
They are both permanent and fragile,
the ashes and oil that imprint us forever
and yet disappear by morning,
foreheads rubbed clean.

Holy Week

He rides the hosannas
into the city, the jubilant song
an invitation, his name.
And then from alleluias
to ragged cries
spilling over the full cup
he has taken.
In darkness God lives the silence,
feels the grief, the questions,
the absence
until one tiny taper remains,
a whisper of first light.

"Death is the mother of beauty"

"Truly I tell you: today you will be with me in Paradise."

Jesus's hands are splayed
against the wood,
held fast, but each small
twitch of pain makes more pain.
Breathing is a task.
But still he breathes.
Enough to speak.

To the desperate cry of unbelief
from one of the crucified,
he closes his eyes.
But to the other who asks Jesus
to remember him,
he offers paradise. Today.

Paradise. So hard to grasp
amidst the clutter
of our days.
Could it be real? we ask,
so afraid it isn't.

But still we can imagine:
the scent of a garden of tomatoes,
the tiny prickles of soft rain,
the warmth of small breezes
on redeemed bodies.
The abundant fruit
and none forbidden.
And time for poems,
wrought in light
so shining we can finally see.
And time for music
in new tempos

and the euphonies
our earthly ears
could not take in.
And peaceful hours,
history finally dead.
And the clouds of witnesses,
not always seen but felt,
their multitudes
never crowding,
always standing,
sparking light,
sitting, even reclining
into the plush of grasses,
sometimes beside water
that seems still
yet moves like breath.

But one poet of the twentieth century
is incredulous.
He finds abhorrent
a paradise where ripe fruit
never falls, where boughs
hang always heavy in the perfect sky.
"Death is the mother of beauty," he writes.
Nothing lasts. Nothing exists
beyond the grave. Nothing.
And that, he says,
creates the beauty
of the few hours we have.

But there is another way:
this dying Christ our only dying.
Our death behind us
in sprinkled water.

So much we do not know,
but this much is certain:
Christ forgave that thief
and drew him close.
Beauty blossomed
in the dark of Golgotha.
We stand in earth, in dust,
and reach for shapes
we see through mist.
The shapes are real.

I Thirst

Before the nails, the outstretched
arms, the cross, they offered drink,
wine mixed with myrrh to lessen pain.
Christ refused and chose instead

to swallow misery.
But now he cries, "I thirst,"
his mouth as dry as fire,
tongue bloated, vision blurred.

He is drenched with pain,
slick with the sweat of it.
His brain alive with neurons,
uncontrolled. That hypothalamus,

the size of an almond,
pleads, "Drink. Drink deeply.
Don't delay." He is so thirsty,
and thirstier, thirstier

as he loses blood.
This is more than a parched throat.
It is longing, yearning. It is craving.
Christ is a man, and he is thirsty.

Christ is our God, and he is thirsty.
How can this be? The Living Water—
How can water thirst?
And what will slake the thirst of Water?

More than vinegar on a hyssop branch.
He is as thirsty for us as we are for him.
He wants us to let him swallow us.
After all is ready, whenever we gather,

we stand in that long procession
down the aisle. We cannot keep it
from being our turn. Hands deep in pockets
fingering our change or last week's laundry slip,

there is something inevitable
about the way we step up the aisle.
At some point, no matter what,
we're first. And then our hands exposed,

we cup them, a small manger,
and the Host invites us in.
The chalice lifted to our lips,
we drink him and he drinks us.

The Silence

The silence cracks the raucous world in two.
He reaches for the cup, embraces his loss,
He stretches forth his arms upon the cross.
Our boon, his death; our life, his blood; our due
He takes within his side, his hands, his feet, the crown we threw
Upon his head, the thorns that bite his flesh across
The silence cracking the clamorous world in two.

"Father forgive them, they know not what they do,"
He cries, and "God, your name you have made fast
In flesh, my own. My God, why have you cast
Me off, deserted me?"
The answer as he breathes his last,
The silence that cracks the darkened world in two.

The Earthquake

The earth erupts,
rocks split, graves crack open.
Death cannot be contained
on one still cross.
It shatters all that is sure
and stable. It turns
creation upside down
and leaves it cleaved
and in darkness so deep
it might as well be death.

What now is sure?
Predictable? If God
can die, what else
is possible? What
is left to be impossible?

This death has thrust
us into forbidden places,
the temple curtain of division
slashed, the graves no longer
prison to the saints,
now so many lazaruses.
We thought we knew
the story well,
but graves opened
and "God's saints
raised from sleep"?
And it is the Friday
of Christ's suffering?

Is it not too early
for resurrection?
But Christ already
descends into hell
and preaches
to the dead.

These times are liminal,
the not-yet after what
has been left behind.
We are ripe for revelation,
and even though Pentecost
stretches 50 days ahead,
we see the world at this moment
in upheaval, the most unlikely,
the centurion and his men
who oversaw the crucifixion,
maybe even the ones who ridiculed
Jesus, now not so certain
he is not the son of God.
A double negative
speaks for itself.

Easter, Before It's Noticed

The garden in the deep night
after God's rapt silence
has no breath. No echo even
in the vacant tomb which no one
yet has visited, no one seen,
and yet everywhere his breathing,
the turn begins, the blanket
of sunrise in mist stretches
to swaddle the earth,
gouged and waiting.

Easter

In the tomb
his cheek ashens,
the silence stiffens.
When will his cells enliven,
his blood begin its orbit,
his skin pinken?
When will he flex and rise
into the dawn of new time?

He quickens, infused with tempo,
his heartbeat
breaking through the grave's secrets
crushing the silence,
trampling death.

And he rises,
he rises indeed,
light blazing.

Pentecost

Stunned into exotic idioms,
the whole world's alphabets
caught in one room,
they now pronounce earth's farthest,
highest, most remote,
while tongues of white-hot terror
kindle and burn over each head,
the wind a gale of revelation.

The Spirit cannot be stilled.
The Spirit seals the cross
forever and spreads
as fast as light.

Magdalene POEMS

Demons, All Seven

She could not say
more than
a pot of claws,
a cruel jag of glass.
litzangle, mosh, she said,
chugging bad wine,
shrugging, flesh squirming.
scritchel, rolfwangler,
and then,
Jesus Christ.
Was it prayer or curse?

And then the sudden silence,
sun on breezeless waters.
Her eyes still,
the color of sea.
His eyes calm,
the color of earth.
Evenly spaced
breaths.

All seven finished,
collapsed, gone.

Crucifixion

He seemed far away and not so far away.
How could he be far away?
But suffering took him there.
Beyond her.

She watched as if it
were someone else's story.
She would say later that her distance
from him brought it all back,
those times when she had no choice
but to submit to chaos
and darkness chewed her whole.

Resurrection

Afterwards when she tried
to close her eyes
she heard only his cry
to silence, his God.

So she rose in the dark,
set out for the grave.

But the startle of its vacancy.
How to explain this, she thought.
Completely gone—
not even cold flesh
which was not quite nothing.
And here was—nothing.

But then everything.
His sudden presence
still distant.
He would not be touched.
This time, however,
sternum, ear, and breath,
tongue, flesh.

Praise him.

Mary SONGS

Annunciation

Sitting upon the tiny flowers
woven in the grass, she gazes
through the leaves into the sunlight,
listening for the rustle of words
to explain the strange angel.
She is rapt with love.
She will say yes to all
creation. She will magnify
the Lord, knowing the image
does not form without the word.
She will bear the Word.

Nativity

The word she bears is heavy as flesh
and light as hair. She breathes
in the pangs of birth and out
her joy, as this child, borne
of a child, arrives sticky in
skin and delicate of bone.
Immensity in such a tiny form.
She curls around him.

Cana

A wedding crisis—no wine.
Quickly Mary seeks repair
and turns to Christ
to do what he has never
done before.

At first reluctant,
he says no,
but like his mother's
smiling yes to Gabriel,
he radiates obedience.

The water barrels filled,
he lavishes with wine
the wedding feast.
He pours abundance
into each guest's cup.

Mary ponders the wine
of celebration,
coursing like water.
It feels like grief.

Crucifixion

She feels every shard of iron nail
and crossbeam splinter, every thorn.
There is nothing for her to do
but stand beneath the cross
waiting, watching, weeping.
When Christ gives John a mother,
Mary a son, she does not know
that this is not the end.

Resurrection

After the rush of sorrow at the cross
she startles at the here and now of him,
his breathing, the blink of his eyes,
the stretch of his hands,
as she did when he was born.
She would like to trace with her fingers
each scar, each wrinkle, each lock of hair.
Instead she gazes, his time fulfilled
and the kingdom come.

— II —

Libretto for Cantata
"Where can I go from your spirit?"—PSALM 139

SOUL

The crisp of wine upon my tongue,
the spice of orange on my fingertips,
my skin smoothed warm by gentle sun.
I find my pliant pleasures
in the plush of scent and senses.
In this dream of life I stand alone.
I travel with the breeze,
drift anywhere I please.

—— DUET ——

CHRIST

I know you well,
your sitting and your rising,
your thoughts, all the words
you speak or even think of speaking.
Your eyes are closed in deepest sleep.
You dream yourself detached.

SOUL

My eyes are closed in deepest sleep,
I dream myself detached.
I travel with the breeze,
drift anywhere I please.

CHRIST

I shaped you in your mother's womb
and even when you flee from me
I'm there with you.

SOUL

I travel with the breeze,
drift anywhere I please.

CHRIST

You want your world to be your own.
But hidden, my hand leads you.

SOUL

I want my world to be my own.
Whose hidden hand could lead me?
I travel with the breeze,
drift anywhere I please.

———————

SOUL

Sometimes late afternoon
shine turns to shade.
I cannot laugh, can hardly smile,
the shadows silence repartee.
What seemed so glistening, new, enticing,
now seems to ask bleak sacrificing.

CHRIST

Do not despair, my soul, for hope has come,
arrived from hazy distances. Do not despair
for light has come. Do not despair, my soul,
wrapped tight in prison's darkness.
On your tongue there is no word that I do not know.

SOUL

Grass thins, mud thickens my path.
My steps are slow. I'm caught in a dream.
My legs move, shears cutting leather
and then I stand locked still as stone,
I cannot flee your spirit.
Breeze stilled, drift stayed,
Pleasure's lures decayed.

CHRIST

You who all through night to dawn have been crying "O Lord,"
mercy has heard that "O Lord" and has come.
O pain, which has grown old, rejoice, the cure has come;
O fastened lock, open, for the key has come.

SOUL

How can you know me even when I hide from you?
You made me in a secret place?
I was unformed and you saw me?
You created my innermost parts?
This knowledge is too wondrous for me.
Where can I go from Your spirit,
and where can I flee?
If I soar to the heavens, you are there,
if I bed down in Sheol—there you are.
If I take wing with the dawn,
if I dwell at the ends of the sea,
there, too, your hand leads me,
and your right hand seizes me.

CHRIST

Darkness may swathe you,
and the night will be light for you.
Darkness itself will not darken for you,
And the night will light up like the day.
The dark and the light will be one.

SOUL

I acclaim you, for I am wondrously made.
How precious are your thoughts,
O God, how numerous their sum.
Should I count them, they would be more than the sand.
I'm tied to you with silken skeins of love
The wine I drank before, mere taste of feasts above.

CHRIST

You who have abstained, you have fasted from my table,
break your fast with joy, for the first day of the feast has come.
But keep silence, keep silence, for by virtue of the command
    "Be!"
your wordlessness is more meaningful than all speech.

SOUL

Silence is too difficult, my God, I am your own
and as your own I see all those who hate you.
They are my enemies, too. You know them
as you know me. But still the wicked prosper.
Search me and know me.
If there be wickedness in me,
lead me instead on the eternal way.

— III —

Abel Speaks

My brother Cain: soil crumbled in his hand,
crevices and cuticles, nails engrained,
he was dirt, all dust, then mud,
weeding even in the rain.

Those tomatoes red as blood,
asparagus, tender spears,
radishes fat as fists.

I offered my firstborn lamb to God.
Cain, the firstborn, upending
all, offered me. If earth
could clot, it would have.

Ghazel for Middle Age: Eve Speaks to Adam

I am neither the green of an unripe peach nor the fragile
feathers of snow. I am as warm as tossed clay.

You were watching the tailless squirrel on our back-porch rail.
I reached for the toasted crusts to balance there.

All that happens now is repetition. One morning becomes
every other
morning as our past stretches landscapes longer than the path
from the garden.

Eventually I would have reached for the fruit
when it fell from the tree and lay on the grassy mud.

Cumulus and stratus give way to nimbus. Now we pay more
attention
to the horizon as the sun rises gold and pinkens the morning
like skin.

Zola, *Imago Dei*, on Her First Birthday

The dust swirls, did it unfurl
this girl, God's deep yearning
for her, once clay,
now *Imago Dei*?

Reach back to Adam,
in Eden's first mud and mire,
shaped whole but not entire,
given blood and bone
but made alone
with all his intricacies of marrow
and joint, a narrow
cage around his heart,
dreaming Eve and then upending
Eden with sin's smart?

The image, we all know, was smudged.
Was it play? Adam would say,
"Let's put it this way:
I am Eve's father
and her brother and her mate,
the image of God's hunger to create,
a mélange of rib and earth and breath,
at first no death, just promises kept.
God's own. His face was mine.
Mine, his. Mine, hers. Hers, his.
But we ate. And then we wept."

So into this stunned world, Zola
burst, at first indignant
at the dazzling light
after the dark tones
of her mother's heartbeat.
Tiny knob of nose, gray eyes,
a fierce grip, this bright sprite,

her face her father's.
They form each other's image.

This spring, amidst Lent's
dirty snow, the cross's
promise still ahead,
the buds in trees still
tightly wrapped, the year's
potential yet untapped,
the branches filigreed
against the sky, baroque
their arms and fingers
pronged and split,
like roots inverted,
Zola's birthday. She is one.

In her purity of gaze,
delight of play,
her belly laughs
at small dogs' pranks,
she is God's hunger
and his plan, her mother's
longing, her father's yen.
Yet she will know
sin's twilight and its night,
and through it all
though sometimes dim
the gospel light.
We pray she reaches
for this unbroken gleam,
this holy bauble,
as she does her father's arms,
her mother's face,
and safe from harm
there find at least the trace
of Eden, wiping the film
from the dark glass,

to see Christ's face,
enigma, ambiguity,
until he is revealed,
the cross, his grace—
the mirror, resilvered
by his glory,
he alone
making God known.

And Zola, once abstracted
in a Petri dish,
becomes herself,
born flawed,
but still the dream of God,
himself, his image.

Elegy for a Bull Terrier

After Christopher Smart's "Rejoice in the Lamb:
A Song from Bedlam"

For I will consider my dog Maddie.
For she meditated at the back door
waiting for the crunch of tires on leaves,
watching the play of shadows and branches.
For she worshiped on the living room carpet's patch of sun.
For she stretched out in cool prayer
on the wooden floor of the porch in hot weather.
For in her muscled youth she chased
the demon possum from the hedge.
For she loved the spirit of wind in her face
when she put her head into it.
For she ate the occasional ant that strayed close to her bed.
For she curled into a fetus of fur when she slept.
For she sneezed on command.

Thou Maddie of the slack lips, the smooth flank,
the vicious appeal of the serrated gums.
Of the great jaws dripping water lapped
or locking around the bone
or holding the toy cat gently in the cradle of thy mouth.
Thou Maddie of ears pricked as if dipped in starch.
Thou Maddie with paws thick as turf.
Thou, my dog, forever and aye,
baptized by my daughter
in the waters of the bathroom sink.
In thy bath thy most primitive self
on display in pink skin under thin fur.
Thou, the beast in my kitchen,
thy great sides heaving with sleep as thou
lay in front of the roast-filled oven.

Thou dog, cur, bitch.
Thou canine, tyke.
Thou puppy.
Thou only and ever after.
Thou rich dogness mingled with devotion.

Thou then in your life's fast, last moments
Smiled thy teeth on the pleasures of thy bowl,
And gave a benediction to thy favorite snack of crusts.
We raise our glasses to thee, noble beast, and say, "Good dog,"
Thou godly inversion, thou sheer hound.

The Journey

After paintings by Joel Sheesley

At one point the windows were boarded up,
but now even the boards have rotted,
the scrub trees branching wherever they can,
the brambles growing thick around the house.

Into this tangle a man and woman step
into someone else's story, odd and unfamiliar.
Finally, however, it is all the same journey,
these stories, the disappeared residents of this house,

even the trench-coated man and woman,
the singer in the wilderness,
the teenage girl standing in front of her makeshift
shelter, the boy bidding farewell.

They are not people of words, these wanderers,
except for the singer pouring out his song or
occasionally the woman as she directs the man's
gaze to the sky. Usually theirs are quiet murmurs,

muted exclamations. Normalcy amidst disorder.
Their encounters are odd: a man rising
from the water, a skeleton in the weeds,
a trampoline in the scrubby woods.

Exotic, even extraterrestrial, they are foreigners.
They accept what the journey offers and go on.
Only once do they show excitement as they bend
over the tiny green plants with their trowels.

But usually like children they accept,
tripping over a skeleton in an odd corner,
toeing the jawbone as if it were an old beer can,
doing things they have never done before,

but maintaining their equilibrium,
their respectable behavior. In their layered
clothes the world they have found is at odds
with what they know even amidst a few

familiar icons—the TV, an upended chair,
out of their elements, dream-like,
with the branches forming a veil
between words. It is dangerous,

this kind of traveling, and it is inevitable.
The man stands in the tree, his arms
stretched for balance against the branched
trunk, his legs barely holding him upright

in this risky spot. His upper torso says
he is in control. His legs betray him.
The woman adopts the familiar pose.
She lifts the fruit to his mouth and he bites.

The building crumbles, the fences lie
broken, the branches are relentless and
unrestrained. And there they are—Adam
and Eve after the fall, startled, unsure

of whether they should protect themselves
or just stand there in full nakedness.
And the dreamer closes his eyes and imagines
entire landscapes as he fingers one branch from it.

We are always trying to return.

Epithalamion: A Sestina

After the rice scatters
on the walkway, after the crumpled
napkins and strewn cake
crumbs on the carpet, the tinkling glasses stilled,
some half-filled on tables, mantelpiece
and windowsill, then comes the stretch

of time that will hold you stretching
for each other in the quiet scattering
light called marriage: pieces
of time pasted together sometimes crumpling
along the edges but still holding, still
gathering like an iced cake.

Your lives filled with so many still-life
studies in boxes around you: the pieces
of this new life, curtains billowing, the scattered
fragments coalescing, the first sweetness as rich as cake,
the later sweetness stretching
toward children, the happy crumbling

of time itself before the quick crumple
into eternity. And other images: the smooth stillness
in the twilight as you walk, the time stretching,
holding the blinking lights of airplanes, the pieces
of stars falling into the September evening air like candles on a cake
so brief, bright, fragile as the long breath scattering

the fire into the cool air, the stretching smoke trails crumpling
into the still room, the memory of the first pieces
of cake offered to each other, and this first bread before all others,
His body, this stay against scattering.

On His One-hundredth Birthday

For Paul Bouman

This long stretch of years, fast dissolving into the past,
is merely the instant before the conductor raises his baton
before the first stirrings of soil as the green-tipped crocus breaks
    through,
before the images fill the page of the poet
when beauty is no more than a tug of words on the tongue. *Selah.*

Now his one-hundredth summer is blooming, blooming,
and stretches its long stems toward the birthday that marks a century
of beginnings—of liturgies sung and the pure tones of children's voices,
of worship in a place of anthems and cantatas,
of the organ in the choir loft imprinted with his DNA,
its pipes and ranks deft with Bach, with Luther's hymns,
and the psalmist's own harmonies, deep and delicate. *Selah.*

Centuries ago an artist painted Christ stretched on the cross,
the cross a giant lute, the strings the seven heavenly spheres,
their music created by God's hand tuning the instrument,
stretching Christ tighter, tighter until the melody of our salvation
bursts forth from the universe, newly redeemed, restored. *Selah.*

This resurrection is the psalmist's music, the only song he sings
amidst lament and joy, a holy melody, the bread of life his flesh,
his to put on, the Word made flesh his canticle. *Selah.*

Crossings

For Pastor Bruce Modahl on his retirement

Both irises, each fingerprint, our own.
Each strand of DNA, ourself, whose bones
descend from Adam's dust, whose breath is God's.
And we are called by name,
each hair imprinted and the tiny bones
inside our ears.

We have a place ordained and gospel-light
to show our way, crossing our life
with his, each cell so clearly stamped "his own,"
and through him we are lords of all,
yet servants, too, Christ-kissed.

Sola Fide

In the pitiless rooms
stark with guilt and stiff
with miseries
he brings thieves to Jesus
and teaches them to pray.
He, who doubts everything,
reads Romans with convicts.

Two weeks before he dies
he lists his deeds for me:
widows, orphans, felons.
He visits them.
His eyes brim with interrogation.
He believes, he says, without speaking,
that he does not believe.

How much does God desire, I wonder,
outside of actions and intentions
outside of struggle and defiance?

In the deed the spark of faith,
a flash denying his pronouncements,
his doubts, his denials.
A particle, a fleck, a crumb's worth.
It is sufficient.

Solus Christus

For St. John's Lutheran, Wheaton

The baptismal font in this hushed church,
Byzantine in beauty, is a cask of salvation,
filled to the brim, its surface tactile,
inviting the dip of fingers, the sign of the cross.

The liquid stretches like cellophane from one side
of the basin to the other, the water trembling,
spilling over in an intentional trickle.
Alive this water, it is our only death.
Why fear the white pall stretching over the coffin,
its surface silk or linen, its expanse a reminder
of this water, this pool? Under the pall we live.
Already drowned, there is no other death. Christ lives.

Sola Scriptura

This collage of tears and laughter,
wanderings toward promise and much later
what seems the murder of the Promise.
Of Isaac freed and Jephthah's daughter burnt,
of Hannah's prayers and Mary's questions,
the *amens* and the *selahs*, the nails of ark and cross.

In the procession behind the lifted cross,
the Scripture, too, is held aloft.
It shapes us. We hear it, sing it,
plunge into God's saving action through it.

It molds space, creates the paraments,
the carvings, the windows filled with story.
Flames and lilies at the altar, these too
from Scripture. Each image a tale, the gospel

a story linking each person in these pews
with every other one who has held
out her hand for bread, his body.

The book is Word, and Christ the Word made flesh.
The language both complex and simple,
formed between tongue and lips,
pronounced, tasted, incarnate.

Sola Gratia

I thought it would be difficult to do nothing,
but between intensities, that is what a poem requires.
Time at my desk, pen in hand, lavender fountain grass
waving in pots outside my study windows,
the city beyond, construction cranes, planes overhead,
then gone. This is where my eyes go—toward the light—
and I think images, sometimes words, musing into the clouds
and sky, the sound of hammers, sirens.

Writing this poem is a matter of saying yes, of giving in—
and the words imperfect, many cross-outs,
not knowing if words will come at all, and when they do,
never exactly what I had envisioned but filling
in the page which once was void.

Is this grace? Is it always this risky?
So uncertain, so surprising? Does it descend
on those who hunger and trust its coming
like those small birds scratching for seed?

Soli Deo Gloria

For Carl Schalk

The composer's vision lacks centers, he says,
the music he writes must fit into his peripheries.
Even so, God's glory dazzles the scores like an ocean's
pageantry of light. What he cannot see, he hears,
and now in the back seat of my car as we travel
to churches of his early ministry, find organs
he once played and choir lofts filled with ghosts
of voices he schooled, he quotes Milton:
"When I consider how my light is spent."
He has its music already in his head.

We cannot fix our gaze and see it all through close
scrutiny in full light. We must catch it in a sideways
glance, tilt into it, and snatch it at an angle.
Otherwise we are blind to it, too dazed by this world
to take it in. We work with these few images
and music heard only by those whose vision
is too dim to see. God's glory is rampant and stretches
us to heaven. Our reach is short. Our toes grip earth.
But we have glimpsed reality and heard its music.

— IV —

What I See on My Terrace When I Write Poems

When the building went up
twenty feet from my window,
I planted hydrangeas that grew
as tall as children,
their heads lush with blossoms,
their tender necks willow stems
nodding in the breeze.
In the dark their outlines
barely visible but dipping
and bowing all night
and in the morning greeting me,
sleepy heads,
a still life never still.

Now freckled with snow,
the heads dried and brown,
whipping the wind,
spastic and fitful,
yet still they cling,
wind rustling
through sere petals
and fleshless skulls,
moving, moving
against the background
of glass and steel,
the balconies across the way
cocooned for winter,
these fierce dark heads
the image of wind,
the visible pricklings of cold,
fewer now but still unbroken,
valiant moppets,
their progeny lurking
under the skin.

What the Butcher Knows

How to dismember, how to separate the fat,
how the muscles stick to the bone, how to detach wings,
how to loosen joints, how to smack pink coils into a paper boat.

He knows about the insides of things,
tucking the neck into the hollow chicken,
stuffing sausages into translucent socks.

Probably also he knows what to do with feathers,
brains, hooves. Wrapping packages of prim chops,
he sees beyond today. He knows how things
turn out if they are not snatched up.

Response to Donne, 2020

On a huge hill,
Cragged and steep, Truth stands, and he that will
Reach her, about must and about must go,
And what the hill's suddenness resists, win so.
—JOHN DONNE

The poet wrote
of circling Truth,
approaching
on a slant,
indirection best
for steep approaches.

But now
the words weigh
us into entropy.
The breath of lies
thick as clay clods,
the tongue glib,
words spewed like water
from a spitting faucet,
a twist a scatter.
No traction
on that hill.

Hushed, we alert
like hunted game deep
in their dens, so silent
even breathing
is mute.

Real Presence, Moon?

Silk saucer,
Runnels and lilt,
Lyric devoid of breath,
Fickle yet faithful costumer,
You are massive at the horizon,
A silver sliver as you wane.
Mostly at night but some
Times, you changeable
Waif, there you are at
Morning rise.

I know only this, silent coin:
You hide then appear
At cloud's convenience.
Little white rabbit soft
In your light, or stately
Monstrance, blank wafer,
I ask you:
Are you blood
Or mere harbinger?

Against Bonding

It's not that I don't want
that velvety head on my knees,
eyes telling me of the sorrows
of all rescue dogs,
this one leaning heavily
against my legs as she sits
next to the sofa where
I am reading.

Or that I don't want
that sweet, curled-up
lump of newborn tucked
under my chin.

It's just that bonding
sounds too much
like insurance,
like gluing stars to paper
for good behavior,
or all the right answers.

Or too much like wrapping
a box with packing tape
or a uniformed agent
slamming the stamp
on a passport.

So—away with bonding!
Let those babies
and puppies sleep quietly
or give their squeaky little
cries for attention.

I will still watch for them:
their bodies' sleep
like warm sacks of flour
nestled on our laps,
or in the crook of our arms.
Not bonding, not pasting,
not sealing, but fitting well
into the angles of bent
arms and knees.

A Psalm for Moving Up

*On the dedication of new space for the Biblical and
Theological Studies Department*

For decades it was a functional set of stalls down a
hallway straight as a railroad car, each scholar's cubby
windowless and packed, the air a mélange of old books,
dust, coffee, the passage lined with empty chairs poised
for students who never lingered. *Selah.* Now this broad
floor unsettles us slightly as we wander into new spaces as
yet unaccustomed, the paint still pungent, the carpeting
untrod. The books in each office are newly arranged and
precise. They stand upright and perfect. The light expands
through slanted panes or startles through mirrored tubes.
And we watch through glass walls as students, backpacks
thrown aside, water bottles on the stretch of tables, crouch
over books, and look up to consider Barth or Hebrew
verbs or the Trinity or Calvin. *Selah.* This is the place
that moors a college in words enfleshed in the Word, that
schools us in *sophia* and *sola fide. Selah.* These are the
scholars who teach us that light is created out of darkness,
who balance the despair and wrath, the hopelessness of
the Psalms with the certainty and extravagant love of
the Psalms, the stark cries of the forsaken Christ with
the fullness of the empty tomb. *Selah.* Walk into the
branching hallways. Listen to the whirr of printers, the
click of keyboards, the soft conversation of students and
mentors. Think of the always younger faces of students,
these chairs holding them, these walls hearing them, our
prayers now containing them, these windows pushing
their vision, as ours, outward to creation. *Selah.* Let us
pause and remember the future, thinking in the ways
eternity entices us, the present moment here, the past
three floors below, the future as we imagine it, and now the
present moment fast becoming past and stepping every

second into our future and the Kingdom that is already here. *Selah.* Let shared tea and other collaborations, quiet talk and impassioned, let laughter and fervor know these spaces and link us, past and future. *Selah.* We pray God's breath would charge these rooms, unrolling this time, as ready for filling as clean newsprint or blank screens with blinking cursors or the still air before the words are spoken. *Selah.*

Permanent Address: 1956

The leaves slick with rain
     from the afternoon storm,
the small, tough leaves
     mixed with grass clippings
for my doll's salad, her tea laid
     behind the side hedge.

The tiny cherries ridged
     like pumpkins, sour,
the pits almost as big as
     the fruit, the juice sticky
on my hands, dripping
     down my wrists, the pits
a small pile in the grass
     mixed with dirt and ants.

Grandma's anger flaring indoors,
     her apron thrown down.
The continual drone of mosquitoes
     seeking flesh,
the huge yellow insects,
     poison-spitters, Grandpa said,
as he bent over his sprouting
     pineapple growing at
the back door, his coffee
     always warming on the stove,
ready for his back porch
     newspaper and his cigar.
His silence when Grandma
     slammed the door.

I would fit myself into corners
       of the outdoors, wedge
into interstices, find freedom in small
       places, the games more
challenging the smaller
       the playing field,
the games unshackling blood bonds
       to anger foaming and burnt.

Where are All My Lost Addresses?

Those ghost dwellings, temporary,
all of them: the Valdosta green shingles,
the Madrid balcony, the Boston
saltbox, the Long Island cottage—
how many others—the Missouri patio,
the air base cracker boxes in Sembach,

Sumter, Montgomery, assigned by rank,
covered garages to colonels, carports
to captains, parking spaces for NCOs?
The addresses, all twenty or twenty-five,
clattering through my childhood
like a box of puzzle pieces pulled down

from a bookcase, each one a potential link
to another, each one a small snip of memory,
disconnected. These places—where were they—
the couch where I lay, my leg in a cast,
the kitchen with the red-hot water light,
the storage cubicle where we pulled

my mother's costumes from the trunk,
the brittle fronds of the grass skirt,
the mothball redolence of the flamenco dress,
her tap shoes, her ribboned ballet slippers
from that world that whirled her
before our birth. Each time the green silk

curtains unfolding their soft fluttering,
the piano nicked in new places, always
a box of books—*Swiss Family Robinson,*
the biography of Clara Barton—
lost with other toys. Each time unpacking
the painting of the kneeling woman weaving,

her husband standing over her like an intent
buzzard. Each time the china cups gingerly
unrolled from the packing paper
and set inside the maple cabinet.
Then the first day of school,
sixteen different times, the fear
that tightened my throat,
the potent odors of spaghetti
or fish sticks in the waxed hallways,
the first steps into the hushed classroom
staring, staring, the tentative
recess invitation from a classmate

cornered by the teacher. This is what
I thought was natural—the unaccustomed
street corner at night, the spruce dropping
cones, each a small thud on the roof
outside my bedroom window,
the stiffness of the new key in the lock.

What I Thought was Normal

We were constantly driving off.
Dad's sunburned arm resting
on the open window.
The air seared, slugging
through the '55 Buick.

My sister, needling imp.
My brother living
in fire and never burnt.
Sometimes crawling
into the broad space
between Mom and Dad.
Leaning toward Mom.

Mom calm in her skin.
Fragrant like bread.
Dad's tonsure precise.
Ever rank and emphatic.
My sister's intensity
what she could break
by stretching.

We were always
sitting on a UXB.

And yet we were also
walking down the Avenida
del Generalisimo in Madrid
still under Franco's thumb.
My father *paseando*.
Never hurrying.
His voice like a plow.
Pushing me
against all forces
to stand alone.
The gift of independence.

Much later after his death
my mother now helpless.
Unable to deflect.
Unable to placate.
Cancer gnawing at her.
Before anyone knew.

What is normal?
Maybe this is it.
A family in motion.
My mother's injured blink.
My father's flash fiction
of love and bitterness.
My brother's gaze
fists on a stone.
My sister's cheeks
burning her path.
And I, waiting,
waiting for the slip,

both mourning
and celebrating
what I did not yet know.

Mother and Daughter

The water laps against the dock.
My mother sleeps, the window open
To catch night breezes, the shift
Of gears across the lake, a siren,
A train whistle, then its grumble by.

The weight shifts on the mattress
And she is suddenly awake in dreams,
Her mother's pale skin, blue-veined,
Her hair, white and long,
Sitting on the edge of the bed,
Then fitting like the cat
Behind my mother's bent knees.

Her whisper is light as cottonwood,
As insistent as a fly. "I told you I'd
Return to you, tell you all. . . ."

My mother fists the sheet to her skin,
Buries her head in it, straightens her legs
And feels her freedom. She sorts other
Settings for dreams, chooses bright
Fabric, patterned lights, fresh water.
Drifts closer to it.

Mobile Killing Units, Lopuchowa Forest, Poland

The hush in the forest is calming at first
and then not. No songs to sing along this via dolorosa
except Kaddish. I walk on pine needles decades
after thousands were herded like animals to the pit
that is just ahead. The silent whispers of the dead

linger, caught even in the branches of these straight
pines, still sloughing, still seeping into the soil.
Yes, Baumgaertner is written in the death
roles at Auschwitz, Peláez in the archive
of victims and survivors. This is not my story,

each name a blood line, each silenced voice words
unlinked from mine. This is not my story, yet I,
a Jew of the New Testament am stumbling along,
my year-old child clinging to my neck.
For a flash of a second I am aware of one sharp
breath and the beginning of a fall into the abyss.

This is not my story, I keep repeating.
This is not my story.

Sciana Placzu

Kazimierz, Poland

The Jewish headstones broken under Nazi tanks,
the annihilation so complete even death's work
crushed, the testament of lives obliterated.

These headstones now puzzle-pieced to form
a thirty-foot wall, each stone, each fragment
with their menorahs, candles, pitchers, broken

branches, a person in each symbol, a name.
A jagged slash, like lightning, from ground
to full height, dark with shadow like a rent

garment, wide enough to step through
into another world of mist and pine-needled
floor, the forest filtering daylight like looking

through the sheerest organdy, a place to stand
with beauty, a place to stand with beauty
ripped apart like the curtain of the temple
torn in two.

Concentration

"In this connection, it is to be borne in mind
that only cities which are rail junctions, or
at least are located along railroad lines, are
to be designated as concentration points."
—Heydrich's Instructions to Chiefs of
   Einsatzgruppen, September 21, 1939

"The area of the camp is so small that, had the
new arrivals stayed alive for even a few days, it
would have been only a week and a half before
there was no more space behind the barbed wire
for this tide of people flowing in from Poland,
from Belorussia, from the whole of Europe."
—Vasily Grossman, *The Hell of Treblinka*, 1944

The word itself:
to focus
to compress
to remove all
distractions
to create less and less
space
for interruption
to fill the smaller
and smaller
spaces with
more and more.

The word
becomes sinister.

To cut even
that space in half
to cut the half
space by two-thirds.

Packed
into stinking rooms
and then transported
crushed standing
in boxcars
6,000 a day
Treblinka.

The camp map:
storehouse for victims'
property
disguised as a train station
execution site
disguised as hospital
barracks where women
undressed
had heads shaved
barracks where men undressed
"the Tube"—the path
to the gas chambers
three old
ten new gas chambers
the cremation pyres.

Today we walk
the forest path
now level ground
the forest path
the forest path
then the clearing
and the ragged stones
standing, these stones
a compression
a concentration
of heat and pressure
pushed
by the earth's crust

from its core
the stones
the rocks
spaced in the clearing
lined up
a congregation
of what's left
after suffering
nothing but jagged
edges,
the silence
its own Golgotha.

Finding Cuba

i.

The first night in Havana
in the yellow convent of Santa Clara
with a night garden thick
with the ghosts of whispering nuns,
the air heavy as wet linen pressed
through a hand-cranked wringer,
the rooster begins its *co-co-Ri-co-co*
at 3 a.m. and I am awake
and at once inside a time
as hushed as the footsteps
in the courtyard and as unfamiliar
as the blue-barred windows,
their shutters open to the rustle
of papaya leaves.

ii.

Inside the Baptist seminary
in the darkening chapel
the president tells how God
made him into a cook
that first year in prison,
how seven pastors met
for prayer amidst the stench,
the clothes rotting off their bodies
over nine years.

He stands in front of a wall
painted with the clear
colors of Cuba, a landscape
of palms and sea framed
by red plastic flowers and ferns,
where the cross in this Lenten season
is now draped with purple
in my Chicago church.

iii.

I walk in the garden of bromeliads
below the glittering mosaic of Fidel
and the Greek Patriarch, where Mother
Teresa's bronzed form also sits
on a low garden wall.

At night outside the convent windows
the African drum beat of Santería
is sticky heat.

On Sunday afternoons the fan
in the tiny church a hot whisper
on the back of the neck,
shoulders nudging shoulders
right and left, the cups and bread
pass down the hodge-podge
rows to the people standing,
to those sitting on the chancel steps,
to the two men on the windowsill
outside the barred windows.

Outside next to the wall
the flowers are borne on spikes
or hidden in the green funnel,
their inner leaves brilliant orange.

iv.

The plaque in the museum says:
From the people of Peru
to the people of Cuba.
Underneath, a potted palm.
Plant this, they say, with many others
to form a green wall
against the beast from the North.

(*Gusanos*, they now call those who left
Cuba—and their children,
they call *the children
of worms*.)

A wall of sharp palmettos.
A sequestered castle.
The houses outside crumble
into pink and yellow rubble.
She almost wakes
but turning to her other side,
digs her fist into her chin,
the needle prick so long ago
the thicket hatchet thick.

Exhibit

At the Garfield Park Conservatory

i.
Inside the translucent blue sphere
tiny cups catch the dew.

ii.
Globes of yellow glass streaked
vermillion, like slippery
buoys bob and drift
with the minute currents.

iii.
Azure worms spiral in and back,
cooling their color at stem ends
as they reach for light,
more light.

iv.
These among the spineless yucca,
the torch plants and purple
starfish flowers, the shrubby sea
bite and slipper spurge,
the giant carrion flowers,
the polka-dot euphorb.

v.
And more—mouse ears, blood
bananas, prickly custard
apples and living baseballs
amidst Chihuly
rhombohedrons,
spikes and towers.
Which is glass?
Which stems and flowers?

Contrivance

Forced serenity, the boll,
cracked, puffed in lines
stretching straitened rows.
Beauty masking pain,
these stalks soon to be chopped.
The artifice everything
to style, to balm,
to death disguised.

Prickly as sand the crinolines,
stiffened cotton, almost horsehair,
we wore under skirts poufed
into fat peonies of color.
We were proud of their flouncing.
It was parties and dress-up Sundays
when we pulled on their bristling.

The head tilted, the drops one by one
into the child's ear, delicate
in its folds and crevices,
peeking out from shaggy hair.
The ache that felled all play
a drumbeat of pulse and pain,
the cotton stuffed tenderly
into the canal, sheltering the grace
of hammer, anvil, stirrup.

The mortician replaces blood
with embalming fluid and reshapes
bodies with clay, cotton, or wax.
The eyes of the corpse have sunk,
but plumped with cotton balls
under the lids, no one knows
this is not merely sleep.

In Matthew Brady's Photographs

The Confederate dead slump
behind a stone wall at Fredericksberg,
mouths open in mute Os,
legs twisted, rifles stretched
across the ditch of corpses.
In another photo a dead soldier
sags in the trenches at Petersburg.
He looks like he is merely resting,
although the cock of his head has death
written all over it. And here is a soldier
sitting in a deserted camp,
arm bandaged, eyes closed
in agony and exhaustion.

On glass coated with an emulsion of silver salts,
fragile, thinner than windows, the imprint
of negative images, all pain and burn.

After the war, thousands of photos intact,
stacked up in boxes, sheds, barn lofts,
ripe for the building of greenhouses,
each glass pane a negative, each image
held firm within a wrought iron frame,
steady for sunbeam and gathering warmth,
the exotics within "rare, foreign, tender,"
lime trees, variegated oranges, magnolias,
rose apples, sugar cane, bamboo, sweet
bays, geraniums, heliotropes, and jasmine.

And over time, each equinox following the last,
sun scorches those dead, so long dead,
until they fade, fade, disappear,

the glass clear with only hints here
and there of shadow.

And the dead silent as grass,
the wind soughing the clash and simmer
of these images,
voiceless and invisible.

When the End is in the Air

The crack between now and then
Slivers into polished planks
Shaking a box of puzzle pieces
Where, why, when, who?

A narrow cage around the heart
Wiping mist from darkened glass
Catching words in winding stairs
Wide reach, short grasp

How the clouds hang poised and brimming
Why the paint chips fill the dream
When the end is in the air
Mouths filled with dust

My Heresy Poem

It began with a walk,
simple, one block to the shop,
but step by step I wondered
why my legs were heavy,
why the purple line appeared
in the bed of my nails,
then the heartbeat,
as languid as poured wax.

The chief heresy after they attached
the electrodes and connecting
wires was thinking God
was not responsible for,
for heartbeats, that is.

Then dreaming the still
breathing without cry
of that tiny Jesus perfect
and not at all human.

Then behind the oxygen mask,
shredding the trinity, wondering
if that small voice could generate
breath, much less be one.

And finally watching the nurse lay out
the glinting instruments, take
my slow blood, wrap my arm
in the cuff, wondering if I really
needed this journey, this promotion
to the great unknown, to an afterlife
of responsibilities.

I could have laughed, but I saw
my soul, dangling, slight

as a spider's web, and I wondered—
Is this the beginning of an arrival
or the end of a departure?

And why these immolating images
and crumbles of what I always knew?
And where was God anyway?

And I knew then he was in the cardiac ICU
one room over, with a failing heart,
tiny breathing, the blood circulating
so haltingly it could not fill the vial,
the nurse laying out the instruments.

But most of all I knew his reluctance
to move into an eternity of responsibilities.

— V —

Orkney PSALMS

VERSE

*If I say, Surely the darkness shall cover me; even
the night shall be light about me. Yea, the darkness
hideth not from thee; but the night shineth as the
day; the darkness and light are both alike to thee.*
—PSALM 139:11–12

Matins: Riding Eastward—Summer Solstice
12 a.m.

It is midnight, Orkney, and mid-summer, and the sky
Has not yet found its deepest sleep.
It will not tonight, as I hurtle your way.
But still three thousand miles to go,
I am six hours east and the sun is so bright
I lower the shades.
May God of light who is light fill our midnights
Like a sun that never sets.
Make our darkness disappear.
Or at least, Lord, make our shadows
Brilliant in your light.

Lauds: An Italian Chapel on an Island in Scotland
3 a.m.

Two huts transformed by war prisoners
Into the beauty of filigree, *trompe-l'œil*, holy space,
The Queen of peace holds the Child gently,
Olive branch in his hand. The cherub
Painted nearby sheathes his sword.
This war is long ago now but still we ask
How can we have savagery and beauty at once?
Praise Christ who cries forsaken from the cross,
Suffering and beauty manifest,
Death's ravages and God's repair.
Guide us, O God, to depths and heights
Beyond the facile.
Help us to see your light in blackened skies,
Your love in the peaceful shade of night.

Prime: Orkney
6 a.m.

Treeless. The fields are green velvet, and withering
Wind whips out to sea and more sea.
It churns the cairns, broughs, lochs and voes.
It calls the mighty orca, otters, puffins,
Razorbills and auks.
The wind speaks, creating praise
On this island of birdsong, heather
Feeding the sweet turf for a thousand years.
God breathes into every bud and bramble.
His spirit hovers over the waters,
And the small waves lap the banks,
The wind strengthening as water slicks rock.
Open our ears, Lord, to your voice
In wind and water. Open our eyes
To light pouring into crevice and cave,
Silent illumination.

Terce: Skara Brae
9 a.m.

The sky, the sea, the rings of tall flat stones.
And now Skara Brae, "haunted by time"
One poet says. But morning shimmers
Here as it has for ten thousand years.
At the center of each Neolithic house,
A hearth surrounded by stone cribs
For sleeping. Maybe for dying.
On the green knolls uncovered by storms,
These ruins. We gaze, the ripeness
Of dung in the air, a cow bellowing
Across the field. These ancients
Used seaweed for fuel
Until sand covered their homes,
The sea salt poisoning their fields.
How small they must have been
To walk through these doorways
Without stooping.
How small we are, O God,
Accept our prayers for grace
Of such immensity that we will know
Eternity in our short span.

Sext: Lamb Sermon, St. Magnus
Noon

At St. Magnus
The preacher speaks of lambing.
She has no herding dogs.
Her sheep know the lilt
And timbre of her voice and come
Into the fold when called.
Born shivering, her tiny-faced
Lambs, so weak on new legs,

Often in March snows,
Are wrapped in miniature Macintoshes.
They curl into her lap.
A hundred ways a lamb can die,
She says. But when they live,
They know each others' faces,
Each one distinct, at least
One in every bunch disobedient,
A troublemaker, always the wanderer.
O God, we listen for the bell or thunder
Of your voice. We await your rescue
And the summer shearing.
We ask that you lead us to stand clean
And shorn before the guileless Lamb,
In midday shine.

None: Maes Howe

3 p.m.

To enter Maes Howe one bends
Like a supplicant and shuffles slowly
Forward into the dark tomb,
Following the same path the sun
will take at Winter Solstice, when light
Overcomes the darkness and the dwindling
Days begin to lengthen.
Praise the God whose
promises warm to summer on a cold and sunless day.
Praise the one who comes, his infant face
Ablaze with love.
Praise the Lord of budding light.

Vespers: St. Magnus, the Lighting of Lamps
6 p.m.

We stand nearest the bones of gentle Magnus
Buried in a pillar, and in the chancel
Watch a folk singer, out of tune,
Practice for a wedding.
Gravestones on the walls of the nave.
On one: *He lived beloved and dyed regretted.*
On another: *Death levels all. Remember death.*
Our prayers rise as incense to you, O Lord,
Our Creator. Hold out your palm, O God,
So we can curl inside it
As you stroke us to life,
Your breath as substantial as clay,
Your touch as light as dust
Suspended in a solitary beam
Of setting sun in this dark church.

Compline: Ring of Brodgar and Standing Stones
9 p.m.

The ring of stone towers, flat rocks,
Marks the earth with mystery. Their makers,
Their movers, gone, the only traces the cairns,
The broughs, and tools of stone and bone.
But we know, seeing the Ring's skyward reach,
That they, too, felt slight next to the Almighty.
We kneel, our God, in front of majesty,
Our posture both chosen and helpless,
Sin-stunted. Your glory, our only wealth.
Your Son our only Sun.
Praise to the God who rounds the days,
The seasons. Praise fullness,
Time completed and begun again,
That we may know you now

And also then in life so firmly anchored
In the mud of earth but reaching
Toward the light so real
We feel its glance upon our skin.

COLLECT

*Almighty God, in shadowy places your radiance
sets fire to night and darkness becomes light. Make
us a steady sheen, reflecting the glory of our Lord
Jesus Christ.*

COMMENTS ON THE Libretto for Cantata: "Where can I go from your spirit?"—PSALM 139

This Cantata was commissioned by the Boston Symphony Orchestra to honor the retirement of principal oboe John Ferrillo, who wished for a piece based on Psalm 139. The composer, Michael Gandolfi, envisioned a Cantata similar to J. S. Bach's dialogue Cantatas. The text includes lines from the psalm and a few lines from the thirteenth-century poet Rumi.

COMMENTS ON THE Orkney PSALMS

The ghosts of Neolithic tribes seem to haunt the air and water and land of the Orkney Islands, off the northern coast of Scotland, where the summer solstice brings bright midnights and the winter solstice is deeply dark. "The Orkney Psalms," written on a trip with my husband, Martin; Rebecca Schalk Nagel; and her father, the composer Carl Schalk, during the summer of 2016, explore the mysteries, the landscapes, and the archaeological sites of the islands, celebrating the lives that have inhabited the place for 8,500 years, and the Creator of those early peoples and their land. The Orkneys are not just geographical phenomena. They are islands which provoke questions, curiosity, reverence, and awe. They lead us to prayer. With that in mind, Carl Schalk composed a suite of choral pieces from the last few lines of each of my poems. Some of the Orkney sites in the poems will be unfamiliar to many readers, so I offer these notes.

"Lauds" describes the chapel built during the Second World War when Italian prisoners transformed two Quonset huts into an ornately decorated place of worship.

Skara Brae is an archaeological site of Neolithic homes near the sea, uncovered by the wind blowing away the sand that had hidden them for thousands of years.

St. Magnus is the cathedral founded in the twelfth century. The bones of saints are buried in one of the pillars of the church, the gravestones on the walls providing an additional *memento mori*.

Maes Howe, a Neolithic tomb mound built 5,000 years ago, where on the winter solstice the sun follows the narrow tunnel at the entrance to illuminate the back wall.

The Ring of Brodgar, similar to Stonehenge, is comprised of massive stones arranged in a circle, reaching heavenward.

ACKNOWLEDGMENTS

The author wishes to thank the editors of the following publications in which these poems have appeared or are forthcoming, sometimes in slightly different form:

Anglican Theological Review, "Solus Christus" | *Animal Companions, Animal Doctors, Animal People* (University of Guelph), "Elegy for a Bull Terrier" | *Christian Century*, "On his One-Hundredth Birthday" | *The Cresset*, "What the Butcher Knows" | *Crosswinds*, "In Matthew Brady's Photographs" | *The Image of God in an Image Driven Age* (Intervarsity Press), "Zola, Imago Dei, on Her First Birthday" | *McMaster Journal of Theology and Ministry*, "Three Poems from Poland" | *The Night's Magician: Poems about the Moon*, "Real Presence, Moon?" | *Poems for Ephesians*, "Poem for November" | *Presence*, "Magdalene" | *Reformed Journal*, "Sola Scriptura," "Soli Deo Gloria" | *Relief*, "My Heresy Poem" | *Saint Katherine Review*, "Exhibit" | *San Diego Reader*, "Permanent Address, 1956" | *Spiritus*, "The Journey" | *Time of Singing*, "Advent," "Christmas," "Epiphany," "Pentecost" | *Valley Voices*, "Contrivance" | *Vineyards*, "Mary Songs" | *Wheaton Magazine*, "A Psalm for Moving Up"

I also thank my perceptive and encouraging editors at Paraclete Press, both Robert Edmonson and Jon Sweeney. Jennifer Lynch and Charity Olsen were extremely helpful in dealing with design and web issues. Rachel McKendree provided invaluable advice and prompts as publicist. I owe a huge debt of gratitude to my dear friend composer Carl Schalk, who would have been thrilled to see both "The Orkney Psalms" and "Mary Songs" in print and who always kept me focused on the things that matter most in my liturgical poems. He is now living in the resurrection in perfect harmony. Michael Costello, Cantor of Grace Lutheran Church in River Forest, Illinois, was the inspiration for "Advent," "Christmas," "Epiphany," "Ash Wednesday," "Holy Week," "Easter," "Pentecost," and "Crossings," all of which he set to particularly haunting and moving music. Bruce Modahl has been an enthusiastic and discerning reader of my poetry for several years, and I appreciate both his support and his insights. And the most astute reader of my work has always been Martin for over fifty years. John Donne writes (with my emendations), "If we be two, we are two so/ As stiffe twin compasses are two,/ Thy soule the fixt foot, makes no show/ To move, but doth, if th'other doe."

This book is dedicated to my four grandchildren, London, Zoe, Cayd, and Zola. May they live and grow in grace.

IRON
PEN

O that my words were written down!
O that they were inscribed in a book!
O that with an iron pen and with lead
they were engraved on a rock forever!
—JOB 19:23–24

Outcast and utterly alone, Job pours out his anguish to his Maker. From the depths of his pain, he reveals a trust in God's goodness that is stronger than his despair, giving humanity some of the most beautiful and poetic verses of all time. Paraclete's Iron Pen imprint is inspired by this spirit of unvarnished honesty and tenacious hope.

ABOUT PARACLETE PRESS

PARACLETE PRESS is the publishing arm of the Cape Cod Benedictine community, the Community of Jesus. Presenting a full expression of Christian belief and practice, we reflect the ecumenical charism of the Community and its dedication to sacred music, the fine arts, and the written word.

SCAN
TO
READ
MORE

Learn more about us at our website:
www.paracletepress.com or phone us toll-free at 1.800.451.5006

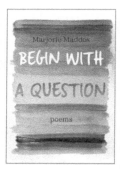